THE MOON'S JAW

The Moon's Jaw

by Rauan Klassnik

Black Ocean

Boston · New York · Chicago

BLACK OCEAN
P.O. Box 52030
Boston, MA 022205
www.blackocean.org

Library of Congress Cataloging-in-Publication Data

Klassnik, Rauan.
  The moon's jaw / Rauan Klassnik.
      p. cm.
  ISBN 978-0-9844752-7-8 (pbk. : alk. paper)
  I. Title.
  PS3611.L38M66 2012
  811'.6--dc23

                                    2012033936

FIRST EDITION

—A Corpse Or A Gun—Her Bra's—Half Off Face—
—Glowing—& Frozen—Like She's Sliced—
—Her Throat—

. . . failed sparks of blood . . . recited . . . quietly . . . from memory . . . Like the beads of a prayer. Or the knots in a flagellant's whip . . . & then, a great power & calm takes hold of me . . . & I'm like a God . . . A ball of cells, seething, inside its host . . . A lone source of light . . .

CONTENTS

Scraped—Up, Over the Trees. & the Howling. Never Bigger—Or Smaller. Night: After Night. Cold as a Fingernail.

IN SHADOWS

She pulls me along by the cock. & we're tearing our clothes off.
& the stars bend down & sniff us: An old man, deaf, blind, & mute.
& behind him—Over the bed—Dozens of photos. & in each
one—We're in a forest. & in each one—We're cradling a baby. A
baby like a crane, on fire—Rising, Up, Over, the Alps. Screeching.
Our souls. All of us.

Deformed w/ light—& slick w/ milk: Suicide's cunning, tragic, & warm. A Baby—Or a Dog. It leaps up at you: & licks at yr face. Its face is scarred. Teeth broken. & bruises—Like sunshine—All down its back. You hold it up—Again & again: & slice its throat.

—Mouths Of A Whore—Spiced Up—Diseased & Sore—
—Expanded W/ Pleasure—& Pissed Down My Face—
—It's Like The Plague—Holding Me Together—A Madman—
—Scratching Her Ass—Up On A Balcony—Scabbed—
—Lobsided—Cunning & Swift—

& now, some lined up ghosts—Behind each a soldier (SS, of course) w/ a gun in his cold white hands. & they've kneeled them down now. Heads arched forward. (Shadows, Twisting—Into, Each, Other. Grinding—Starved. & Blue. Crawled—Up, Out, Of, a Pit. Whining. & Trembling.) & they've fired up thru their heads. Brains—Splattered—All over the pavement. That's how we're fed.

—Prayers Ought—To Be Castrated—Stand—
—In The Corner—& Taste My Piss—Huge & Silver—
—Condors Vomiting—Stiff Gorgeous—Pregnant Ablaze—
—Splintering Back—Into My Pale—Veins—Like Angels—
—W/ Long Red Hair—

She borrows a knife—Circumcises her son—& walking away, throws him high up over her shoulder. Want to know about miracles? Or the triumph of the human spirit? I found her—A rabbit's foot's clutched in my heart like worms & shit—& ground her down into the finest dust. A body's soaring up thru the clouds. The moon—Raising a finger to his lips. We nibbled: & gnawed. & mounted each other in cold blind light.

—Stars & Cockroaches—Gathered Around Us—Millions—
—Of Them Untying—Unlacing—Bones & Pulp—Sucked—
—In A Shower—Of Kisses Carved—In My Heart—
—My Cock In Marble—Swirling Monstrous—
—Galaxies—Lying In Wait—

In a circle of girls—*Her* girls—who pose for her. Filthy: & moaning. Naked. On their knees. W/ their hands behind their backs. "I hope you don't mind my love," she says. The sky's ash. The grass too. The flowers. Her teeth: & her tongue. "O, I don't mind," I say. "I don't mind at all."

—Undressed—Hands In Our Hair—Creation's—
—Groaning—"Do You?"—"Do You?" & Yes!—I'm Raining—
—Up In Me—Lights—Etched In My Blood—
—Louder—& Louder—In Spirals Of Dark—The Same—Old—
—Lights Full Of Whores—

An old woman—No! Look closely & see! She's just a child—Bends over to pick at a small gray flower. This might be happening inside a star: Or the shadow of a tank—Topped w/ a soldier. & look, he's floating on down! & look, he's reaching for her! & look!—I've thrown up all over them! Marble, Tequila, Rotted, Flapping. In the wind. & its green-pink seizures.

—Quietly—Up On A Balcony—Wheeled Round—
—I'm Kissing Myself—& Shaving—& Jerked Off—
—In My Mouth—Thrust Up Like—A Dog In Heat—
—The Sidewalk—Rolls Up—Birdcages Cracked—In Me—
—Swinging—In & Out—

An old man's riding his daughter's breast milk. She tries to rise—
Boned in light. But he's dragged her down: & pulled out her heart.
Her skull. & her spine: Floods of red surging smoke: Crows, falling,
like bits of ice. Or a Peacock—Rattling its universe: Blue & green.
Like the skies over Auschwitz: Welcoming us. W/ arms wide open.

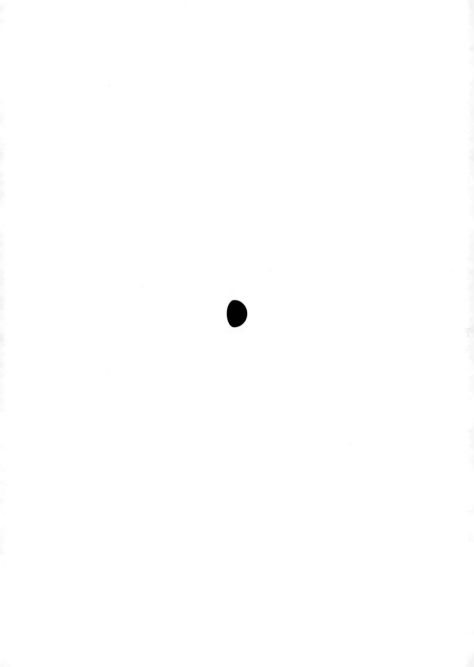

A MAN & A WOMAN

Under the moon's tightening wrists—Leaning down to pet yr dog,
you looked up at me, & shot the dog in its face. We fucked. & we
fucked again. & when I came to you were sucking me off. Like my
brain—Slow & aching. A rat's in a maze. It stops—Grows—& it is
the maze. Futures—Stopped. Coins, chips—& rippling, cash. All—
Bone white.

A bride, young as a Barbie, holds on to an opened watermelon. Like a bee—Its gold wings shuddering. A man & a woman climb out of a car—& come, bristling, towards me. Like a machete: Or a cake knife. Orderly. & jagged. Soothingly. Vicious: & raw. I have learned to die. & not to. I am filled w/ silk.

—Encrusted W/ Emeralds—Stinking Ditched—Boiling—
—I'm On The Back—Of An Elephant—Rubbing—My Pussy—
—Blooming Magic—Night After Night—Flowers—
—Birds & Sun—Whore's Meat—Hanged—On My Soul—
—Glowing—& Moaning—A Stabbed Cosmos—Drooling—

Curled up against each other we licked & sucked till we came splashing in each other's faces. A chimp's running down thru the rain: Like fish, hanged, ecstatic—All the ways to scream! Suddenly he pulls into a doorway: Where a woman's undressing. Like the heart's taut shadows: Light's dribbling in thru the frozen leaves. Soldiers: & music. Swarmed: In our hair. Down our faces. Columned. Spired. Domed.

—Scraped Into Rain—The Sea's A Spider—
—Dancing In Shit—Spliced Open—Like Skulls & Skin—
—In My Throat's Semen—Towering Up—Breasts Sprouting—
—Groaning Barking—Screaming—A Shore—Tumbling Down—
—In Drops—Whitening—

In Vegas—Lilacs, boiling, cool, & dark—You begin to eat my ass: Wiping yr mouth, from time to time—& glaring up at me: Like a Vampire, a Lion, a Shaman—Swaying, bubbling, seething: Down into every nerve . . . Cold white shores swaying . . . Till—At last— You slide in a finger . . . Then two. Fist! Elbow! Shoulder! Head! . . . & you're inside me: & yr breasts are my breasts. Yr cunt—My cunt. Yr slow dark heaving mouth—My slow dark heaving mouth.

—Grazing Deep In Me—Deer Stand Up—Like Clocks—
—Chirping—Chirping Gargoyles—Between Our Legs—
—I'm Two People—Me & A Woman—Abruptly—
—Then Playfully—Passionately—Adam & Eve—
—A Plucked Bone—Wreathed—& Teething—

Waves. & Flowers. Revolving. In black lace: Gurgling. You're pushing me back down on the bed now. & you've got my wrists above my head. & you're eating me out—Licking up between my breasts. It's dusk. Lights, Wound, Up, In a Spiral: Hooked—Thru Me, Like Gut, On, Fire. Yr grip's tightening. I'm sinking: Like fish—In cool shade. Birds, like planets—All ripped up.

—Sailing By—On A Calm Blue Sea—Pale & Slow—
—I'm So Young—& So Fresh—& I Can't Stop Coming—
—In A Taxi—Crushed In A Lobby—The Phone's Ringing—
—It's My Voice—& It's Beautiful—"You're Beautiful"—
—I Sigh—

I'm dead—But alive. & we're in kind of a 69 position. To heal me. The side of yr head: Against my cold, black panties. "Please, be careful," you tell me. "Please." & it feels like we're kissing—& it feels like we're making love. A woman, dead, in childbirth. Tiny bones, resting, still, between her legs.

—Paws Outstretched—Gray As A Pile Of Rubbish—
—Too Bright To Lick—The Wind—Thru The Statues—
—Grows Rarer & Rarer—Broken Clanging—
—Glinting Quickening—An Orchard—Of Flowers—
—Swaying—

& the sun goes red. & the sun goes green. Dolphins moaning in gangrene. Waves—Heavy as tetanus. & we're led thru the twinkling beads: Sat down. Jerked off. & done w/. "You can take it," she growls. "Or leave it." Climbed, Up—From the sea. Melancholic: & hot. Clawed away—In twilight. The moon's jaw. Blue. & darkening.

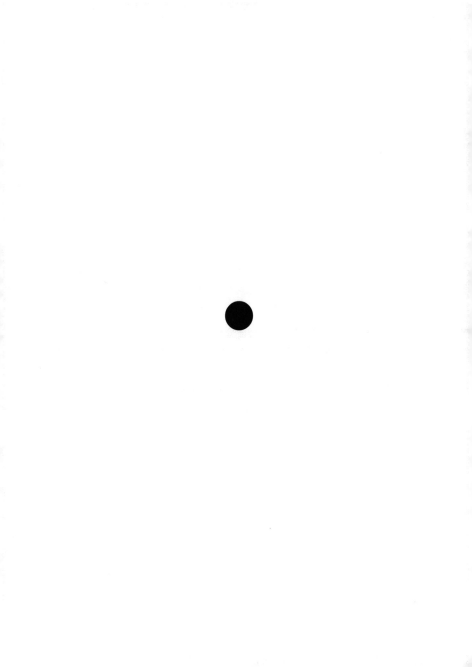

THE GREAT POET

—Spinning—Glorious Handsome & Weeping—
—Like A Fetus—Slow & Heavy—I'm The Beginning—
—Clinging To Myself—An Animal I've Skinned—Carved Up—
—Crawled Into—A Dinosaur—Changing Colors—
—Slashed Into Light—

Again, & again: Out of the cradle endlessly rocking. Again, & again:
The great poet strides on to a headland—Red petals falling—
& hangs himself in a tree. As bright as the 4th of July: A girl's
voice—In leaves of fire: Arced overhead: From sea—To sea.
Dribbling, down, on us all. Sunsets. & all that trash.

—Dementia Melancholy—Softly Enameled—
—I Don't Give A Fuck—It Lights Me Up—Crushed—
—Like Stones Circling—Flies In A Rage—I'm Lifting—
—My Mask—Scratched Slashed—Nailed In My Mouth—
—A Sun's Thick Blood—Smears—My Wounds—

When you aren't crying: Or cursing me out: You're begging me to cum on yr tits again. I should never have promised I'd stay here: In a prison: In a theater—Eyes—Collapsed into one dead eye. But, finally, the sun: Like a horse, molten rock, as it rises up to mate . . . The light: Its shadows. Our brains, charred, w/ pollen: Rats, gorged, on coke . . . A whore: Posed, in a field . . . Or a kid, kite-high, looped in rubber (Soweto: Gasoline, fire, in a tire!). I'm on my knees again. Wilted. & black.

—Millions Die—But Here I Am—Yesterday—
—Today & Tomorrow—Cupped In My Hands—Rotted—
—Sperm & Milk—Touching Each Other—Like Flowers—Born—
—Feeding On Carrion—Draped In Heat—It Tastes—
—Heroic—

Hacked down. & skinned. A pile of bones. The world just eats & eats.

Vultured color—In darkness, throbbing. Like a child, spun, round & round. I'm
rising from the bath—& covering myself w/ a towel.

I'm lost. & I'm lost. But, I'm in a room w/ the president. & he's on his knees: A long, thin curved penis. & I'm talking him into orgasm. "Hey, you're that guy," he whispers, "who shoves souls up into his crotch." Buildings shimmer, violently, outside the window. Like a fetus—Slow & heavy. "Yes, that's me," I sigh. "Yes, that's me." Bits of cum are falling everywhere.

The lights have all turned yellow. I am shaking. I am strong. Under the trees—
In shadows: & in lights. A woman's playing the violin.

In jungles—Chained together—Crumbling. In the corners of my brain: & my mouth. The sun's behind you. You are tall & dark. I am crying. I want you to fuck me crying.

—In Slices—Of Bayonet Music—I'm Sewing You—
—Into A Skull—You Can Fight It—Or Be My Slave—
—Primitive—Dark & Bony—Spewing Religion—Gasping—
—Inside Of Me—The Core Of Me—Epileptic Unfurled—
—Guts Ripped Swans—Bulls Blood—Light—

Laid back—Wrapped in a thin red towel. Like ships leaning together licking each other's shoulders. A voice: Kneeling. In weeds—Panting.

You did up my hair—Holding it tight like I liked—& even tighter as I cried out suddenly: Glancing over at a fetus in a jar. As though it could save me—Crawl back into me—& fill me w/ milk. Children, hands locked, dancing all round my gleaming body. You painted me: & jeweled me. Posed me in bed: Dead, but reaching up still. Lips parted slightly. Shining blue.

I am no one. I am nothing. But I start to glow: & to thrum. I am blown up w/ light. I am draped in every tree. All the shores are dead w/ me.

—Hard & Calm—Closed—In My Eyes—Mouth Elbows—
—Soldered Bones Broken—Like A Horse—It Just—
—Pours Out Spluttering—Bubbling Splashing—A Ghost—
—Up On A Throne—In Blue Decay—Oozing Pigeons—
—Twitching—Down Thru—My Toes—

Warmed up, the flies—Butterflies included—Take to the air. This works great at weddings: But funerals are better. Like kneeling in front of the Mona Lisa: Or gondoliering Venice. A glitzed eel: Contorted. Stiffening. Yawned: Thick. Glaring. & red—Peeled, back. Thru—The mirrors: Thru—The wind. A wide, deep, music, rising up. Snails, brightening, every tip.

—A Woman's Crouched—W/ Her Legs—Drawn Up—
—"You've Killed Us"—She Screams—Panting Sweating—
—Held Up Between—My Teeth's Mirrors—& Chandeliers—
—Spat Out Souls—Trickling Down—My Broken Nerves—

& now's the best part, smeared—Thick & bubbling—On to the rocks around you. A plague of frogs . . . The quiet in death's fat heart. Time's crushed neck . . . Like the feeling after you've popped a zit—Sunrises stirred together in a shy anesthetic: A thousand—All just quite right . . . Winters—Of pale blacks & blood: A flower— Huge, gold, & magnificent—Grown up out of yr stomach . . . & scattered, out—Thru, the dark.

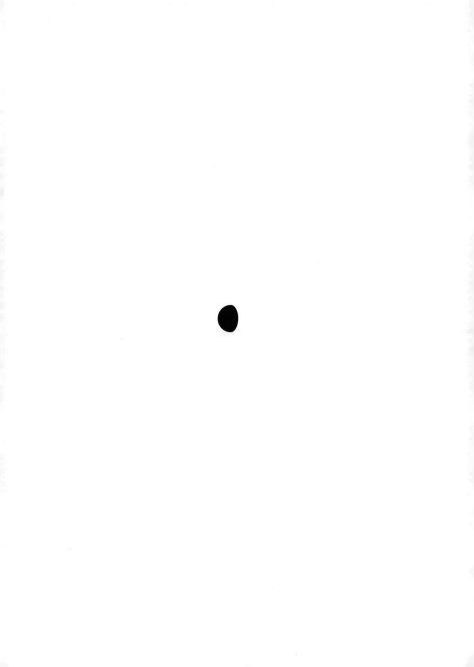

SUICIDE: THE GIRL

She crept up behind you: & tied yr hands behind yr back. Pulled yr pants off. & started to jerk you off—Fields of clouds, striped red & yellow, springing up all around you. This, anyways, is what you told the police. & how it hurt: & how it really hurt. Till she was bent up against a tree. A temple, reclaimed, by the jungle. Bit—By bit.

In San Miguel I saw a Quinceañera girl. In a big white dress. In a bright red car. In front of an old, magnificent church. Strangers stopped to take her picture—Or paint her portrait—& she waved at them w/ tremendous poise. Like a steel doll. The square behind her, filled w/ balloons & tall sticks of candy.

—Disappearing—In A Field Of Poppies—
—Eternity's Torn W/ Sunsets—Beautiful & Charming—
—Rushing All Over Us—Pulled Up Thru Her Bruises—
—Mussing Her Curls—Peeling The Hooks From Her Back—
—A Goddess Delivered—Jerked Under—Ribs—Buckled—
—A White Yacht—

The stars glimmer like small blurred-red flowers—& lying next to you, she presses a talon against her clitoris . . . Swollen, like fire . . . & rips up . . . Thru her navel. Chest. Neck. Teeth—Clenched. The top of her head . . . & it's all so brilliant—& chic—She just absorbs it—Lying back, arms, spread . . . Like the waves of a crucifix . . . Her eyes brighten. Hardening: Paled . . . She bleeds out—A carnivorous flower.

—Jarred Like A Rat—In Bed—W/ A Hard-On Sparkling—
—Petals Shred—Dazzling Round Its Head—"You Have Such—
—A Kind Face"—She Says—Like Making Love—
—To A Corpse Scratching—Its Face—In Its Blood—
—The Universe—Blossomed—In Every Way—

At the end of her show—She steps forward. Spreads out her arms. & proclaims: "I'm all yours, boys." & we're devouring her. The Queen. Of Desert: & of sex. Of doctors: & of blindness. Of mania: Mummies—& the stillborn. Clouds, swollen w/ light: Hispaniola: Great, big boats. Fortified towns: Choked—In smoke. A Queen—Wrapped in bear's fur: Staring down on us. & down on us. We're devouring her. & devouring her.

—A Match—You Fall Into—Vomiting—
—Darkening Pulp White—& It Pulls In Yr Tongue—
—& It Strips You Down—Swollen Great—Black Hills—
—Whitening—A Blind Suicide—Hanging—Chained—
—Up In A Tree—

She moans like you're doing it already—But she holds back. Or seems to. & you force her. & she submits—Towering, Up, Over, You: Sheathed in metal. Like stars in twilight. & then, leaning down—Whispers: "Come, baby, come." As she tears out yr heart—& touches yr face. Church bells: Raining. Blackbirds. She stares, down, on her bright pink knees.

—Singing—Tiny & Precious—Whored Up W/ Slaughter—
—She Tells Us—To Fuck Off—The Hotel's Empty—
—Lakes Of Snow—Laughing & Dancing—Up Into Thousands—
—Finally—She Lies Still—A Saint Stretched—
—Thru W/ Wire—A Tear—

Rusted—& foaming: She lies back, dead, against a herd of pillows. Like a pearl diver sucked down by a pale octopus. Light's blowing thru our bones like tumbleweeds. Waves wash up—Fish pant. & she's right in my face: Like a message, launched: Up, into space. Cold. Futile. & throbbing. Forever.

In The Sky

You stick out yr hand. & I put mine in it. Waves, clouds, & ground—All sucked up around us. &—It's time: A mask w/ a hole in its forehead: Like blossoms: Or tubes between us—Flaring. A plum—Glutted w/ music. & bruised—W/ light. Resting—In the warm, soft grass.

A man & a woman—Clutched together—Tattooed on the sky's long, twisting arms. Like a shining ghost—Devouring its creation. & I'm the man: & I'm the woman. & I'm the cure for cancer. Sweating—In labor! The eternal—Arrival! Trucks—& trucks—Of it, kneeling, stretched, over, a dog's head. Raw—In dazzling, muscled color.

—Jogging Along—In A Dream—Unlit Swaying—
—In Thick Welted Iron—I Heard—Whimpering—
—Tongues Wailing—Stiffening & Headless—
—Fused & Feasting—Smashed—Together Ignited—
—Rivers—Bury Us All—

Egrets clamped down on us: W/ their necks between yr breasts: & their beaks in my mouth. & then slump forward: Cold, red, & white. Like cathedral meat. A child's fingering a hole around us so big it's fired thru the sun. The universe. Our souls. Horses—Hooked thru the neck. Terrified, gaunt, & blood-eyed. Trickling, back, down, into our wasted bodies.

—Bursts Of Laughter—Gored & Gashed—Screaming—
—Flapped Up Thru Our Bones—A Rabbi—Unrolls The Torah—
—Dripping—Like Ballerinas—Chiming Off Groins—
—Buttocks Swallows & Snakes—All Swirled—In Iced—
—Hallelujahs—

The suns are crows, burning, austere, & frazzled—& we're turning round them, each one of them—Like a pig on a spit . . . Our bones & fat—Dripping & snapping, each—Other, In Half, Repeatedly, Imploring . . . "The Messiah has come!" . . . "He has come!" In spirals of boiling semen . . . A toilet—Filled w/ roses . . . An ice cube in a starved man's mouth.

—We Formed A Circle—& Became A Mountain—& Crashed—
—Everything's An Orgasm—Growling Frozen—
—Mauled & Writhing—Furious & Ecstatic As We—Sail On—
—Flush W/ Birds—Doors Abandoned—Hooves—
—& Green Mansions—

In surges of seized-up shadows—Rolled, burned, knifed, & gleaming—We're an ocean full of rocks grinding back into our bodies . . . As we pant, moan, & coax out a last few drops . . . An owl's flying, up: W/ a baby in its claws . . . 'cause, again, it feels like, we've been   delivered.

—Flies Cooled—Brightening—In Our Mouths—
—Like A Child—Killed—In A Car Crash—& Faded—
—To Colors We Fuck—Crooning—Thick Tongued—
—In All Our Beauty—Like Angels—Drizzling—
—Kicked Pale—In The Teeth—

"O, it must be possible," you sang—As you rummaged thru the pale stacks: Of shoes, boots, sandals, etc. A girl surrounded by ghosts: Millions of them—Sucking their thumbs . . . "O, it must be," you sang . . . In veins of marble . . . "O, it must be" . . . As we floated up, calmly . . . In a column of perfect bubbles.

—Rocks Singing—In A Pool Of Rocks—We're Nothing—
—Bits Of Meat—Wolf Stink Rising—Gutted—
—Night After Night—Till The Last—Moon's Blown—
—In A Pile—Of Rust—

A scratch of blood's dribbling, down yr cheek, as you lean back for leverage. We're crawling towards each other. Like standing in the Coliseum: A tiny fish, sliced open, under a great big silver sky. There's no blood in us! Moons—Eyelash thin! I am hard: You are wet. There's no way out. But we don't stop trying.

NOTES:

Much of this is pieced together from bits & pieces of some erasures ("Imperfect Erasures") I made one hot, humid Mexican summer. The more they corrupted & decayed the more beautiful & flexible they became: Long after we'd left that boardwalk, that plaza, that sea: Those moons, full or not, that suffused our house.

I owe much to my readings on disease, sex, religion, violence, God & the Holocaust: especially the godlike Tadeusz Borowski. Also, all those twilights I stood in the shul in Emmarentia & prayed for the dead w/ my dad. & the sense & lust in me that screamed "No! No! No! . . . "

Some of this (versions or bits thereof) originally appeared in Coconut, Htmgliant's *Sunday Service*, Eleven Eleven, Typo Magazine, Dusie, Mud Luscious, Radioactive Moat, Action Yes!, The 5-2: Crime Poetry Weekly, Tarpaulin Sky, Sub-Lit & *Ringing* (a chapbook from Kitchen Press).

—Why—Am I Laughing?—Why—Not?—